Tales of t]
Cornish
Smugglers

John Vivian

Tor Mark • Redruth

For further information of all the titles in this series please visit:-
www.tormark.co.uk

Published by Tor Mark, United Downs Ind Est, Redruth, Cornwall TR16 5HY
This edition 2012
© 2012 Tor Mark
ISBN 978 085025 429 7
Printed by R Booth Ltd, The Praze, Penryn, Cornwall TR10 8AA

Foreword

Despite the inroads of commercialisation, there lingers in many Cornish fishing villages and coves something of the romantic atmosphere of the old smuggling days, when sea-booted figures shouldered heavy tubs of spirits up steep cliffside tracks on moonless nights to the waiting horses above, running the gauntlet of Revenue cruisers, Preventive boats and the coastguard to get the precious 'goods' safely landed and away.

Inevitably, much nonsense has been written about the smuggler; and the truth, as is so often the case, proves to be far more interesting than far-fetched fantasy. The selection of smuggling stories given in this booklet are all true, and have been derived from authentic contemporary sources.

The smuggler emerges from them neither as a criminal nor a hero, but as a courageous, resourceful and enterprising character, who did no one – except the Chancellor of the Exchequer – any particular harm, and benefited his fellows not a little in providing them with cut-price luxuries. Left to his own devices, he was the most harmless of men; it was only when Authorities sought to curb his activities that he showed how ready he was to defend what he regarded as his legitimate interests.

Most of these stories belong to the early nineteenth century – that period when smuggling was in slow but steady decline, and when the violence and bloodshed of earlier times had been somewhat moderated.

Traditions of such incidents as are related here are still handed down in a few local families – though they are not always for the ear of the inquisitive stranger.

'Rigging out a smuggler' published in 1816. The artist (Rowlandson) has got slightly carried away; bladders would have been used – rather like oversized hot water bottles - not small wooden barrels – see page 45 for the story

Beacons in the night

Every smuggling operation was carried out by two teams of men, who had to work in the closest concert with each other to achieve success – those on the ship which brought the contraband goods from France, and the shore party who helped to land and convey them safely away to their destination. The latter task was often the more dangerous, and required much physical effort, particularly when heavy casks had to be carried up high and steep cliffs. This explains why it was sometimes necessary to employ large numbers of men in the landing party – as many as a hundred or more – to get the goods removed expeditiously from the coast before the onset of daylight.

The greatest danger which the ships had to face came from the Revenue cutters which constantly patrolled the coasts of Cornwall and also from the Preventive boats, which usually operated closer to the shore. But even if they eluded these hazards, there still remained the possibility that their boats, on landing, might run into an ambush should the Preventive men have discovered that a 'run' was to be made at that particular place.

The existence of such an ambush would usually be known by the shore party, who might quite well have been disturbed by it themselves. The recognised manner of warning the boats approaching the trap with their precious cargo was by lighting a fire on shore. For this purpose, a beacon of furze or other suitable materials was prepared in advance, and some of the party were detailed to kindle this should the need arise. So common was this practice that it was made a punishable offence to light a fire upon the coast as a signal, and several instances are recorded where men were brought to trial for this offence.

At Cornwall Lent Assize in 1828, John Brown, John Dunstan and William Borlase were indicted for making a light to give notice to their associates at sea, in order to prevent the landing of a smuggled cargo. It appears that on the 9th of March Samuel Gammon, boatman of the Cawsand Coastguard station, was on duty on Rame Hills, near Porlorn [Polhawn] Cove, about a mile and a half from Cawsand. At three in the morning, Gammon and another boatman called James Dyer hid themselves in a furze brake near Rame church. They saw a fire in the gateway, and three men came into the field with lighted straw in their hands, and made lights in three different directions.

Gammon ran across and caught Dunstan, who was coming from the gateway where the fire had first been seen. On seeing three smugglers running across the field pursued by Preventive men, Gammon let Dunstan go and joined in the chase. Eventually three prisoners were secured. Before the fires were lighted, a vessel had been seen standing in for the land.

To take another example: at Cornwall Lent Assize in 1825 a smuggler named Spry was indicted for lighting a fire on the banks of the Helford river for the purpose of warning smugglers of the approach of Customs officers. It was proved that on the arrival of Preventive men at the spot where the defendant was found, some straw was ignited, and the defendant cried 'Run! Run! They are coming!' The officers then rushed forward and secured him. Spry admitted the truth of this evidence, but declared he had no hand in lighting the fire; he was merely on his way home, and on seeing the officers approach cried out to the smugglers to run. He handed to the court a testimonial to his good character signed by several respectable persons, but this did not prevent him being found guilty.

During the early morning of December 4th 1831, the French smuggler *Elizabeth*, having on board 338 kegs of brandy and gin and some packages of highly dutiable manufactured glass, appeared in the vicinity of St Ives. Her master was a certain Jean-Marie Yves Creach, and she carried a crew of six French and two British. When first observed from the shore, she was standing into the bay under full sail, it being their intention to land the goods either at Gwithian or Hayle.

The Coastguard at all times maintained an all-night watch from several vantage points in and around St Ives and as soon as Moses Martin, Chief officer of the local station, was told of the craft's suspicious behaviour, he and his assitants immediately went out after her in the Coastguard cutter, together with the St Ives customs boat. However, the smugglers had confederates waiting ashore; and as soon as they realised that the *Elizabeth* had been detected, they lit fires to warn her of danger.

Port of Saint Ives. By Order of the Honourable Commissioners of His Majesty's Customs.

On Tuesday 17th April, 1832, at Ten o'Clock in the Forenoon, will be exposed to PUBLIC SALE, at the Custom House in this Port, the following GOODS, VIZ:-

The broken-up HULL of the vessel ELIZABETH, with her Cables, Anchors, Tackle, Furniture, and Apparel, A BROKEN-UP BOAT; A quantity of GLASS, consisting of a Liqueur Stand, Tumblers, Rummers, Decanters, Wine Glasses, Salts, &c. A number of small Tubs and Slings.

Custom House, St Ives, 3rd April, 1832

The French vessel promptly turned about and put off again. A stern chase then developed between her and the pursuing coastguards. Martin was a sworn and inveterate enemy of local smugglers; and he kept determinedly on the vessel's tail until eventually she was overhauled and captured about six miles from the coast. She was then brought in triumph into St Ives harbour.

Her crew were subsequently brought before the St Ives magistrates on December 13th and fined £100 each, but being unable to pay, they were committed to Bodmin Gaol. Two of them were Cornish: one, called Yellam, from Probus, and the other named Bawden, from Mevagissey.

As for the poor little *Elizabeth*, she suffered an even sadder fate. At that time, to prevent seized smuggling craft from being 'bought back' by their former owners at the subsequent auction and once more used for contraband running, the authorities had the hulls of such vessels sawn into three parts, and their ropes destroyed prior to the sale. And this is what happened to the *Elizabeth*. A copy of the advertisement put out by the St Ives' Custom house in respect of the disposal of this vessel, is shown on page 7.

It will be seen from this last case that warning beacons were not always effective in enabling a smuggling vessel to make her getaway; but that many were saved by this means is an undoubted fact, and explains why those who lit these beacons were hunted down so vigilantly by the Preventive men.

The drunken miners of Wheall Howell

On April 19th 1825, a Polperro man fishing near the Cannis Rock found, on hauling up his line, a keg of spirits attached to it. Continuing his new sort of fishery, he took on board upwards of forty kegs, and carried them to Fowey Custom House, where in due course the officers rewarded him handsomely for his trouble.

He was not the only lucky fisherman during that time. For weeks the whole coast between Polperro and Fowey was in a state of disorder in consequence of a large quantity of smuggled liquor found along the shore. In particular, the agents of Wheal Howell, a mine to the eastward of Fowey, were greatly inconvenienced thereby, with the miners continually in a state of drunkenness. On April 20th all the men belonging to the mine assembled, and by stratagem, in pairs, succeeded in getting underground where they had concealed a keg of brandy, and drank themselves to such a state of intoxication that it was with extreme difficulty several of them were brought to grass [surface].

In the evening, a party of seamen of the Preventive service arrived with their officers, it being suspected, as a great many tubs had been seized by them in a small cove near the mine, that the miners had concealed some underground. A diligent search was made by the Preventive men through all the workings, conducted by the mine captain, but it did not appear that more than one keg, now nearly empty, had been taken underground.

Too much credit cannot be given (stated a contemporary report) *to the humanity with which the officers and crew of the coast guard stationed at Polperro, performed their duty and it may safely be stated that, but for them, several of the miners would have lost their lives. A great many idle and disorderly persons had assembled, particularly a miner named Thomas Sincock, who said he belonged to a mine named Wheal Sally, near Bodmin; he refused to go until one of the Preventive officers drew his sabre and compelled him. Notwithstanding the inconvenience and loss it occasioned the mine adventurers, it has been judged advisable to discharge the whole of the men, and every endeavour will be made to discover the men who first brought the spirit into the mine.*

This instance of a bal knocked as a result of tapping a keenly lode of spirits must be unique in the annals of mining.

Casualties of the ' Trade'

The economics of smuggling were the same as those of any lawful occupation – that is to say, the trade could only be considered viable if a profit was shown after all losses and contingencies had been allowed for. Superficially, the profits were huge, merely because of the evasion of Customs dues, but a variety of factors tended to reduce them considerably. In the first place, customers expected to pay less for smuggled goods than for articles purchased legitimately, so that if the 'free trader' did not offer a substantial discount, he was unlikely to make a sale.

A more serious matter, of course, was the risk of losing both ship and cargo by seizure to the Revenue authorities when attempting a 'run'. Such seizures were frequent, and must have put many a smuggler out of business. In areas where the Preventive service was corrupt, the risk of seizure could be greatly minimised by offering bribes – often of a liquid nature – but the cost of these then represented another major item on the debit side of the ledger.

The furtive manner in which smuggling operations were necessarily conducted could lead to another serious kind of loss. Instead of boldly entering a safe harbour in daylight, as an honest vessel could do, the contraband runner had to lurk, without lights, upon an open coastline at night in order to land illicit cargo, with all the dangers that that entailed.

A wreck caused in this manner occurred close by St Michael's Mount on October 24th 1822. A smuggling boat was totally lost there with her crew and cargo after nearly completing a 'run' from France. Four bodies were later recovered. On the boat's stern was painted *Rose of Gweek*, and the name of her owner, James Richards. A watch, marked James Gilbert, was found on one of the bodies.

The victims were removed for interment by their relatives. They were those of William and John Gilbert, brothers; and of William Chaffer and William Curtis, the latter being a man of some property. The *Rose* was said to have been formerly the *Waterloo*, of Truro.

Another shipwreck, less tragic in its consequences, took place a few miles away, by the Wherry mine at Penzance, on September 13th 1837. She was the *Friends*, of Falmouth, late of Porthleven, and, like the *Rose,* had been over to France for contraband. She had had a most terrible voyage, her crew exhausted and expecting her to sink at any time. Of the 57 tubs of spirits she was carrying when she struck, one was broken open in the wreck and 52 were recovered by the Coastguard, another four being supposed to have been stolen.

The attack on the Helford Customs House

Early in the month of September 1840, a vessel called the *Teignmouth* was seized by the coastguard of the Coverack station. Outside the vessel were attached 133 kegs of spirit, a mode of concealment which had long been practised on the East Coast, but never before attempted in the West Country, the length of passage from France to Cornwall making it inconvenient. The mode of capturing this vessel was also most unusual, not to say amusing. It appears that, on approaching the land, the smugglers saw two men on the beach, whom they asked to assist them in drawing ashore the kegs. The men consented readily; but then, when the goods were safely landed, drew their pistols and declared that they belonged to the Coastguard. The smugglers were too few to resist, and so both the brandy and the vessel were taken.

This happened within the Customs port of Gweek. The prize was therefore taken to Helford, where the Custom House for the port was situated, and the brandy was deposited there in the Queen's warehouse. The smugglers seem to have felt their loss very keenly – the more so, perhaps, on account of the circumstances under which the seizure was made – and they resolved upon the rescue of their property.

Accordingly, about one o'clock on the morning of September 18th, about thirty or forty of them assembled at Helford, and, forcing their way through several doors, reached the cellar and carried off all the kegs save three. From the wheel tracks left on the spot, the robbers appeared to have brought waggons to carry off their booty. The man and his wife who lived at the Custom House for its protection heard the smugglers at their work, but were afraid to raise any alarm; and, indeed, their doing so would have been quite ineffectual as there was no other house within half a mile or more. It was said that no such offence had been committed in the county for many years; and great concern was expressed at the desperate and lawless spirit which it revealed. One cannot help thinking that the authorities themselves were somewhat to blame in the matter, for siting the Custom House so vulnerably in so isolated a place.

Smuggling at Mullion

In general, the south coast of Cornwall was much preferred by smugglers for landing their goods than the north, for a number of reasons. Not only did it involve a shorter sea journey from France, but it provided a greater choice of secluded coves and landing places, as well as sheltered bays in which kegs could be safely sunk, for subsequent recovery. The district around Mullion proved particularly suitable for such operations; so much so, indeed, that it was said that scarcely any family in those parts was not connected in some way with the 'trade' during the eighteenth and early nineteenth centuries. Long after the practice had been stamped out, Mullion men used to speak proudly of the day when they were engaged 'in the smuggling service' showing how little disgrace was attached to this occupation.

Several good stories have been preserved concerning smuggling at Mullion. On one occasion, a Mount's Bay boat, commanded by a certain 'Billy of Praow', ran ashore at Mullion Cove with a cargo of French brandy. The *Hecate* gun-brig, then stationed in Mount's Bay, sent a boat to the scene, and the smugglers, being taken by surprise, abandoned their prize, making scarcely any resistance.

Later, however, local people collected in large numbers, broke into an armoury, and supplied themselves with weapons and ammunition. They then went to the cliffs and, firing upon the gun-brig's crew, compelled them to relinquish their booty and return to their ship. Many of the most respectable of the local inhabitants participated in this lawless affair; though they were threatened with prosecution, the matter was somehow hushed up.

One of the most celebrated local smugglers was known as the 'Spotsman' – a name derived from the fact that he was in charge of the cargo, and selected the precise spot on the coast where it was to be landed. He had made many successful runs, but on one occasion the Preventive men, learning of his departure for France for another cargo, resolved to capture him on his return. A Revenue cutter cruised off Mullion, whilst the shore force was augmented by some men from other districts.

Eluding the cutter, however, the Spotsman arrived off the coast in the Mount's Bay boat he had engaged for the run, and quietly landed his cargo of kegs below the cliffs at a place called 'The Chair', between Mullion Cove and Predannack Head. Sending off the boat with two hands, he and another man went to meet their friends at Predannack, whom they found in the act of lighting a large signal fire to warn them of the 'enemy's' presence. On being told that the

'Cousin Jacky' (cognac) was safe on the rocks at The Chair, the party hastened there, and, on their arrival – so quietly was everything done – actually heard the thump of the bow of the Revenue cutter's gig as she ran into their own empty and retreating boat.

Hastily removing as many kegs as they could, they hid them for the time being in an abandoned mine adit, leaving the remainder on the rocks. Meanwhile, the Preventive gig had carried off the smugglers' boat, and, taking the two men on board, made her fast to the cutter. They then returned to the cliffs to search for the contraband, but though they actually landed within a hundred metres of the remaining kegs, failed to find them, and returned in disgust to the cutter. The smugglers returned to The Chair and shouldered all save two of the kegs left there, these last having somehow broken from their moorings. As they were ascending the cliff with their burdens the first light of dawn showed the Revenue cutter lying off at anchor, with their own boat made fast astern. A fishing boat was later sent out from the cove which, under the pretext of 'whiffing', recovered the last two kegs of 'Cousin Jacky' from the rocks.

The man who is credited with having finally put down smuggling around Mullion was Lieut Drew, the chief Coastguard officer for that district. He learned that one night an attempt would be made by a group of smugglers – including the Spotsman – to make a major 'run'. As the lieutenant, accompanied by one of his men, was watching the suspected spot, he came unexpectedly upon a party of smugglers awaiting the arrival of their vessel. These men immediately dispersed into the darkness, discharging a few random shots as they went. One of these whistled between the coastguards but, undeterred, they descended the cliff, and in the cove below found a rope attached to a rock and running out into the sea.

They hauled in the line until a tub of spirits appeared, then another and another, until no less than a hundred were drawn to shore. Pistol shots and rockets were used to summon the other patrols, who quickly seized the tubs and chalked the broad arrow upon them. The Spotsman had the mortification of observing all this from behind a rock, where he had hidden to escape detection. Crowds collected the following morning on top of the cliffs to watch the hauling up of the tubs; 'and a solemn silence reigned among them while the Coastguard's men, as if performing mystic ceremonies, struggled to and fro up the rocky gorge bending beneath the weight of their spirituous burdens. Among the spectators, the smuggling interest was well represented – they had come to take "a last, a long, and sad farewell" of the precious kegs so shortly to be consigned to the dark recesses of the Gweek Custom House.'

This was the Spotsman's last run – and only a fortnight later the Preventive men seized two smugglers and six tubs during another attempt to land contraband. The absolutely final occasion – as far as is known – when the 'free traders' made an effort to land contraband at Mullion took place at Angrowse Cliffs. Lieut Drew and his men disturbed a party who had settled themselves snugly behind a hedge, and as they gave no satisfactory replies to the Coastguard's challenge, an order was given to search them. As this was going on, the whole area around was suddenly illuminated by a great blaze of light – the firing of a furze beacon to warn off the expected vessel. She thereupon made off, having dropped her cargo overboard. This was afterwards crept up by the Mullion Preventive men, assisted by the crew of the Penzance Revenue cutters. What may possibly be a contemporary account of this incident appeared in the *Royal Cornwall Gazette* in April 1840. It reads:

Mullion, near Helston. – Since the affray between the Coast Guard and a party of Smugglers, which occurred here on the night of the 3rd inst ... the Dove *and* Sylvia, *Revenue cutters, with their respective tenders, and parties from the Coast Guard stations at this place, Porthleven and Coverack, have continued to seek for the smuggled goods, which were sunk on that occasion: and after great labour and perseverance, they have at length succeeded in creeping up 98 tubs of foreign spirits, which have been taken to the Custom House at Helford, in the port of Gweek. – We do not hear that any of the smugglers have been apprehended.*

An anker in the garden

Whilst for the smuggler the time of greatest danger was when he was attempting to 'run' his cargo ashore, and distributing it to his customers, the 'goods' could never be considered absolutely safe until they were actually drunk, or otherwise consumed, as the following instance shows.

In April 1822, John Real and other Customs officers attached to the port of Falmouth, had seized 59 tubs of spirits in a barn belonging to a man called Rogers at Point in Restronguet Creek. They left them there in custody of an officer called Pascoe, and went to St Mawes for a boat to take them away. On coming to the barn they were told that some of the tubs of spirits had been carried off, and accordingly proceeded to search the adjoining fields and gardens. In a garden belonging to a person called Nicholls, the keeper of a public house at Point, Real found a jar containing 3½ gallons of brandy and half an anker* of gin. As he was about to remove the cask, a woman came out of the house with a shovel in her hand. She appeared at first disposed to offer some resistance and made several unsuccessful attempts to break the jar.

Rogers and about twenty other local people then came on the scene remonstrating with the officers for acting as they had done in digging up the woman's garden; Rogers said that if they had acted in the same way on his land they would not escape 'with whole bones', and that they had no authority to search in this way. After some further altercation, Real showed Rogers his authority, but the latter alleged that it did not permit him to search on land, adding that he was himself a constable. In proof of this, he produced his staff, and

* An anker was a small barrel containing either 9 or 4½ gallons of spirit.

said he could call all those persons present to assist him in preventing the Customs men from acting as they had done.

The crowd, swelling in numbers, began to press upon the officers and having got the spirits into the boat, the latter embarked and pushed off from the shore, amidst abuse and a volley of stones. The officers thereupon fired their pistols over the heads of their assailants.

At the following Lent Assize, held at Launceston, an indictment was brought against Rogers, charging him with having, with several other persons unknown, obstructed and assaulted John Real and other Customs officers, in the execution of their duty. Elizabeth Nicholls described how she was sowing seeds in her father's garden when the officer came to search it for the missing tubs of spirits.

He thrust a stick into the ground all over the garden, and found a jar and a small cask under the earth. She was about to leave the garden, but the officer presented his pistol at her to prevent this. Inevitably, she knew nothing of the spirits being in the garden until the officer discovered them there.

The jury found the prisoner guilty on the assault charge, but not of obstruction. It is not known what penalty was imposed – doubtless it was a light one.

Desperate affray with smugglers

On the morning of November 19th 1828 a run of contraband spirits was made at Swanpool, near Falmouth and carried inland. At about midnight, John Prior, the Customs riding officer of Falmouth, and his opposite number at Mylor, named English, fell in with a band of about thirty smugglers. The arrival of the officers at first threw the smugglers into confusion, and three horses and sixteen tubs of contraband spirits were seized. Prior and English expected little further resistance but the 'free traders' subsequently rallied and set upon the officers in a body. Shots were then exchanged, the smugglers firing first, and a regular fusillade ensued. English was beaten senseless with clubs until he was thought to be dead, and the men succeeded in carrying off all their illicit goods. The usual advertisement was subsequently circulated in connection with this affair:

CUSTOM-HOUSE, London, 20th November, 1828

WHEREAS it has been represented to the Commissioners of His Majesty's Customs, that in the Night of the 19th November, instant, a large party of Men (armed with Pistols, Bludgeons, and Knives) in the act of conveying Smuggled Goods from the Coast, were intercepted by two Officers of the Customs near CONSTANTINE CHURCH TOWN, in the Parish of CONSTANTINE and that the said Officers seized from the said Persons several Horses laden with Spirits, which had been run on Shore without payment of Duties: and that after the said Officers had so seized the Horses and Goods, the Smugglers with force and violence rescued the same from them, at the same time feloniously assaulting and ill-treating the said Officers, so that the life of one of them is despaired of.

The said Commissioners are hereby pleased to offer

A REWARD OF £300

to any person or persons, who shall discover or cause to be discovered any one or more of the persons concerned in the said Outrage, so that he or they may be apprehended and dealt with according to Law, to be paid by the Collector of His Majesty's Customs at the PORT OF FALMOUTH in the said County of Cornwall, upon Conviction.

A Cornish jury will never convict a smuggler

So runs the old saying, and if never is perhaps too strong a word to use if we are to conform with strict historical accuracy, its general validity was strikingly illustrated more than once.

One case was on the night of March 28th 1835 when Richard Stevens, of the Coastguard Station at Fowey, doubtless acting on 'information received', went to Lantic Hill, accompanied by Walter Harper, another Coastguard. There they lay concealed in some furze bushes near Pencannon Point. At half-past eleven they heard a party of men, numbering a hundred or more, and saw that about twenty of them were armed with clubs. The coastguards then lost sight of them for a while, the night being so dark, but a short time later they heard the smugglers on the beach below. Stevens thereupon sent Harper to Polruan for assistance. Soon afterwards he fell in with three men carrying tubs; these they dropped, and escaped towards their own party.

Stevens went to the edge of the cliff but could see no one below. He then heard coming the party Harper had summoned and fired his pistol to guide them. It was answered by these men – five in number – who came up and joined him. They then set off after the smugglers, and, on overtaking them, demanded the goods. The latter replied, that if they touched a man or tub, they would murder all six of them. Each carried a tub on his back, some also having a tub in front, with a rope across their shoulders; all had sticks in their hands. After a violent struggle, in which Stevens was struck on the head with a club and laid out unconscious on the ground, the Coastguards managed to take three prisoners and later another two.

Meanwhile, Lieut Ciddell, commander of the Revenue cutter *Fox*, on learning of the affray, had sent a party of men to Lantic Hill. These found the advance party with their five prisoners in custody, and these were taken in charge and put on board the cutter. The *Fox* subsequently delivered 118 tubs containing 484 gallons of brandy, which had been seized, to the Custom House at Fowey.

The five prisoners were brought to trial at the Cornwall Summer Assize, charged with 'assisting others in landing and carrying away prohibited goods, some being armed with offensive weapons'. The prosecution pointed out the injury that would be sustained by the legitimate trader if the Revenue laws were not strictly enforced; that if any party assembled for the purpose of carrying away contraband goods, such assembling would be felony, and all would be considered guilty, whether armed or not. The defence endeavoured to persuade Harper and five other Preventive men to admit that the thick sticks carried by the smugglers were such as were frequently used by country people as walking sticks; but this they refused to do. The Rev Richard Buller was called to testify to one smuggler's good character – whilst about a dozen farmers from Lanreath and St Germans spoke in favour of the other prisoners.

In summing up, the judge enlarged on the nature of the offence with which the prisoners were charged – an offence alike 'injurious to the community, and to the fair and honest dealer'.

He observed that if Stevens had died, and all who were present had been detected, they would have been guilty of murder. Despite all this, the 'impartial' Cornish jury, disregarding all the evidence laid before them, returned a verdict of not guilty, adding that the sticks were not offensive weapons. As a result, the lucky prisoners were accordingly ordered to be discharged.

The pseudo smuggler

During the month of February 1837, a person calling himself Giles, of Padstow, made his appearance on the north coast of Cornwall, where he visited several cottages along the cliffs telling the occupants in confidence that he had just landed a cargo of smuggled goods nearby. He asked them to tell him how he might remove these in security, and promised some of the liquor for their advice and assistance, The advice was of course readily tendered, and the assistance almost as readily promised; the story was whispered about, and, tempted by liberal offers of spirits, people from different villages were ready to lend a helping hand.

However, the stranger told them that all was not yet ready; he had to call on various friends in the neighbourhood to learn when and where to remove the tubs. Unfortunately, he was in no great trim for taking long excursions into the country; his shoes were worn out and damaged from clambering over the rocks while landing the goods, and he would feel obliged for the loan of a better pair. His shirt, too, had been saturated with salt water, and he would feel equally obliged for the loan of a new one. Again, while he had plenty of foreign notes, cheques and bills, having just landed from Bordeaux, he was quite out of English money, and the loan of some loose silver would be just as acceptable as the shirt and shoes. In this fashion he was given a good meal, provided with new clothing, and given sufficient money for his needs.

Thus equipped, he set out to find customers for his smuggled goods, and returned at night elated with the success of his expedition. The Hotel, the King's Head, the White Lion, and the Fountain, had all given him orders, and he had scarcely passed a beer-shop but would take a tub or two by way of enlivening a little the dull

21

monotony of the kidley. Next morning, at an early hour, operations were to commence; and as a proof that he really had done business on the preceding day a number of horses and a variety of vehicles drove up to the cottage at an early hour. From the owners of some of these, the artful Giles contrived to extract a little cash on account. The morning, however, wore away, and the principal customer had not made his appearance – what could have become of him? It would not do to take away a part without removing the whole; Giles would just step over to find out where he was. He stepped away, but took care not to step back again, leaving his kind hosts minus shoes, shirt and silver, and his anxious customers their cash paid on account.

The most interesting aspect of this true and amusing story is the light it throws on the general attitude of Cornishmen at that time to a self-professed smuggler. Everyone he approached was only too anxious to lend a helping hand. No wonder the authorities found it so difficult to get assistance from the public in laying hands on the genuine article.

Five hundred pounds reward

One of the methods used by the Customs authorities to give some protection to the officers and men engaged in the Preventive service was to offer rewards for information in cases where they had been subjected to any kind of violence. The sums offered ranged from £50 for relatively minor cases of assault to £500 when a serious attack had taken place, resulting possibly in injury or death to the Government men.

Just how effective the system was remains conjectural. The Customs authorities could hardly publicise any payments which they had made, for fear of bringing reprisals upon the recipients by the smugglers or their friends. The impression, however, is that few informers ever came forward in response to these appeals. The 'Free Trader's' greatest safeguard, in this respect, was the general sympathy shown to him by all classes of the public. Everywhere welcomed as a public benefactor, and by none regarded as a criminal, the usual motives of public duty that induced people to volunteer information about other lawbreakers simply did not operate with smuggling.

One should not imagine, however, that the rewards offered were insufficiently tempting. Fifty pounds in the early 1800s was the equivalent of two years' agricultural wages, so five hundred represented untold riches to a poverty-stricken fisherman or farm labourer. Yet, either from fear or sympathy, very few appear to have come forward to tell what they knew.

It is, of course, a question as to how many did know what was going on. Smugglers operated mostly at night, and in isolated places; for this reason, few outsiders could have learned of the exact particulars of any 'run'; on the other hand, it is hard to believe that the members of a small fishing community had no knowledge of the fact that certain of their neighbours were engaged in the 'trade'. However, since the payment of a reward was always conditional upon obtaining a conviction, and a conviction could not be obtained – especially in Cornwall – save by the production of the most precise and detailed evidence, it may well be that few members of the public ever came into possession of facts sufficiently positive to warrant their coming forward.

On the whole, one is inclined to think that the only person who could effectively betray a smuggler was one of his fellows. A grim instance of this is said to have occurred on one occasion at St Just, where a man betrayed his own brother to the gallows, simply for the reward. But traitors of so black a dye as this must have been very few. On the whole, indeed, it may have been that the issuing of these 'Reward' notices was intended merely to act as a kind of deterrent to would-be smugglers by keeping before their eyes the possibility of detection, and by demonstrating the determination of the authorities in bringing offenders to justice.

CUSTOM HOUSE, LONDON, 13th July, 1831.

Whereas it has been represented to the Commissioners of his Majesty's Customs, that on the night of the 6th instant, Thomas Wills, a Riding Officer, and George Pooke and Sampson Wood-cock, Boatmen, in the service of the Customs at the Port of Padstow, in the County of Cornwall, were violently assaulted and ill-treated by a large party of armed Smugglers unknown, whilst in the execution of their duty at Porthmere Cove, in the said Port, in endeavouring to seize a large quantity of spirits, which had been run on shore without payment of duties.

The said Commissioners in order to bring to justice the said Offenders, are hereby pleased to offer a **REWARD** of

£500

to any Person or Persons who shall discover or cause to be discovered any one or more of the said offenders, so that he or they may be apprehended and dealt with according to Law. To be paid by the Collector of His Majesty's Customs at the said Port of Padstow, upon Conviction.

By Order of the Commissioners.
T. Whitmore, Secretary.

Brandy in the ballast

It has sometimes been assumed that smuggling was virtually extinct in Cornwall by about 1840. Whilst the back of the 'industry' had indeed been broken by that date there still remained work for the Revenue officers to do until well into the 1850s, as this incident reveals.

About noon one day in December 1851, Commander Forward of the Revenue cutter *Sylvia*, observed the smack *Wellington*, of Plymouth, off Padstow harbour, standing about eight miles from the shore. Suspecting there might be contraband on board, he stood across to board her, but she altered her course. While pursuing the smack he observed the man at the helm leave his post several times and go to the main hatchway apparently assisting the crew.

In fact, whilst the smack undoubtedly hoped to elude capture, the main purpose of those on her was to destroy all incriminating evidence before she was caught; but in both these objects they were unsuccessful. The *Sylvia* eventually overhauled her, and some of the Revenue men went on board, finding, on the hatchway being opened up, that there was a strong smell of spirits.

Mr Forward found part of the sand ballast quite wet with spirit, which he believed to be brandy. One of his men found the hoop of a cask and part of the stave of a tub. The pumps were tried, and the water discovered to be impregnated with spirit, as proved both by smell and taste. (The picture which this conjures up of a group of Revenue men solemnly sniffing and tasting cans of filthy bilge water surely epitomises the humours of smuggling.) The impression of a tub was also discovered in the ballast. But the most damning evidence of all had been secured twenty minutes before the *Wellington* was taken. This was a tub of brandy floating thirty yards astern of the smack, there being no other craft within six miles of either vessel. The cutter afterwards cruised about, and two hours later recovered eight kegs, of four gallons each.

The guilty vessel was brought into Penzance, where the Collector charged Capt Teed, master of the smack, John Spiller, mate; and the two crew, with having neglected to heave-to on signals being made by Her Majesty's Revenue Cutter *Sylvia*, also with destroying the cargo to prevent a seizure.

The evidence produced being considered sufficient to justify the bench in remanding the crew, they were held for a week, and the Customs authorities in London informed of the circumstances. On December 31st the accused men were again brought before the magistrates, and each sentenced to six months imprisonment with hard labour in the Borough gaol.

The smugglers of Gerrans Bay

Above Porthcuel on the Roseland peninsula lies the village of Gerrans, which appears with its church and spire on the hill to the east side of the creek. A few small creeks branch off right and left from this arm of the Fal, the principal one being on the eastern side above St Anthony's Pool, which extends to within a quarter of a mile of the coast. The ground between the creek and the sea is quite low, and forms the isthmus which connects the bold peninsula of St Anthony with the mainland. It is a fairly easy matter to carry a light boat over this neck of land, and so reduce the distance of passing St Anthony's Head; and this place was once, at least, made use of for such a purpose.

A particularly active Customs officer, who lived at St Mawes, had often been baffled in his attempts to make a seizure from the numerous smugglers around Porthscatho. Whenever these men were busy in Gerrans Bay, they always posted scouts on the hills, some of which overlooked the mouth of St Mawes harbour, so that when the Customs boat went round St Anthony's Head, she was narrowly watched. Should she approach Gerrans Bay, the alarm signal was made, all the boats dispersed, and by the time she came into the bay, everything was quiet.

Realising what was happening, the officer one day took his boat quickly up the river and had her carried by the crew across the neck of land, enabling him to get into Gerrans Bay completely unobserved. He came suddenly upon the smugglers, and secured a good prize.

The strange case of the Letitia of Flushing

In the morning of March 7th 1834, the *Active* Revenue cutter on the Falmouth station was cruising between the Manacles and the Dodman in thick and hazy weather. On its clearing up, Lieut Henry Miller, the *Active*'s commander, observed a vessel about three miles to windward; she was cutter-rigged – a suspicious circumstance in itself! – and was standing north-west, that is, for the land.

After some manoeuvring, *Active* closed with the cutter and hailed her. 'From where have you come?' 'From Flushing.' 'What name?' 'The *Letitia*, of Flushing.' 'What is your cargo?' 'Tobacco.' 'Where bound?' 'Faro.' On being asked whether she was in the course for Faro, Capt Miller replied, 'Yes, by the wind.' He then asked that the cutter be hove to, so that he could send a boat on board.

The commander despatched a boatswain and a boat crew to search the vessel and soon afterwards the boatswain hailed the *Active* to say that he had been prevented from carrying out the search. Capt Miller thereupon sent the chief mate with an armed party to board the vessel, instructing him to take charge, and the *Active* would follow. Thereafter, they both came to anchor off Falmouth.

Next morning the captain and crew of the *Letitia* were brought on shore and taken before the magistrates. The cargo was tobacco, in small packages of 27 kilo weight, plus spirits in three-gallon tubs. All the prisoners were committed for safe custody to the town prison – where, it was said, they were allowed 'every possible indulgence and liberty' – to wait a subsequent trial.

To Lieut Miller and his men it must have seemed that the arrested men would be automatically convicted, for the cutter's cargo was certainly incriminating enough. But they were doomed to disappointment – for the Flushing from whence the *Letitia* hailed was not the waterside village just across the water from Falmouth, but its larger namesake in Holland. And that made all the difference; for not only was the vessel herself Dutch, but the crew as well; and the latter were therefore immune from a provision of the British law which would otherwise have applied to them.

Yet the unlucky foreigners found themselves put to considerable difficulty and expense to clear themselves. Witnesses had to be procured from Holland to prove that they were truly natives of that country, suspicions being entertained that one or two of them, at least, were technically English citizens. When they again appeared before the magistrates in May, the Netherlands' Consul represented the illegality of detaining the vessel, cargo and crew, and claimed the Court's protection for them. The Act under which they were charged stated that *if any British subject be found in any vessel not square-rigged within eight leagues of the coast of England having contraband goods on board in small packages, the said vessel and cargo shall be forfeited, and the said British subject be fined in the penalty of £100.*

During cross-examination, Capt Miller was asked if he had not offered a person named Pascoe £50 if he would try to discover whether some of the party were not Englishmen, but this the captain firmly denied. The first prisoner to be tried bore the curious name of Yander Smith. One of the witnesses from Holland was a tide waiter in the Dutch Customs, who resided at Flushing. Speaking in Dutch, he stated that he knew Yander Smith's father; he was a Fleming and he had known the prisoner from a child.

Seven seamen from the *Letitia* were next brought separately to the bar, and sufficient evidence was given by various witnesses to prove that both they and their parents were natives of Holland and Flanders.

John Fagg, master of the *Letitia*, was then called forward. A Dutch witness testified that he had known the prisoner since he was two days old. The prisoner had resided in Holland all his life. He also believed his father was a Dutchman, as he always spoke Dutch. However, the solicitor to the Board of Customs said he did not dispute Fagg's being born in Holland, but maintained that both his father and grandfather were Englishmen. The defence then submitted that it had been proved that Fagg's father was a burgher of Flushing at the time of the prisoner's birth, and that he was to all intents and purposes a subject of Holland. The solicitor for the Crown, in answer, quoted an old Act of Parliament, which stated that a person born of British parents, although in a foreign country, remained a British subject.

However, the magistrates eventually decided to discharge Capt Fagg; but the vessel remained in detention, and the question as to her condemnation was referred to the Court of Exchequer in London.

This case excited much interest at Falmouth, whose citizens felt some concern at the damage it might do to the reputation of their port. It would, indeed, appear from a superficial view that Capt Miller had acted high-handedly in seizing the vessel after discovering that both she and her crew were Dutch. However, the fact that two of those on board bore the very English-sounding names of 'Smith' and 'Fagg' undoubtedly gave him legitimate grounds for suspicion. Added to this was the fact that Englishmen occasionally disguised themselves as foreigners on a foreign ship in order to evade the above mentioned Act when engaged in smuggling operations. One can only say, in short, that the *Letitia* was an unfortunate and innocent victim of the rigorous preventive measures then in force against the 'free traders.'

'Old Worm's Fool'

On the night of May 31st 1851, a noted St Ives smuggler, Capt James Williams, carried out one of the most daring runs of contraband ever known in Cornwall. He landed his cargo of whiskey, from Ireland, by the old breakwater at St Ives and stored it away in fishing boats pulled up on the shore, and also in the stys of the notorious 'Pigs' Town' which then flourished in that quarter. Late at night two or three waggons were loaded with the stuff, and, exemplifying the truth of the old maxim, 'the more public, the more private' these were driven openly through the streets of the town to the eastward.

This bold action might have been completed without ever attracting the notice of the authorities; but, as luck would have it, a Coastguardman happened to be sitting in the parlour of the old George and Dragon inn, which stood in the Market Place. Hearing the sound of hooves and wheels outside he hastily put down his glass and went out to investigate. Seeing the waggons, and realising what was afoot, he endeavoured to stop one of them; but Capt Williams and another smuggler knocked him down, and then bound and gagged him beside the roadway whilst the waggons made good their escape.

At the bottom of Skidden Hill they were met with extra horses, and on reaching the top galloped off towards Hayle and Redruth at a furious pace. After a while the coastguard managed to free himself, and hastened to inform his superior, who lived in the Warren, of what had happened. Without delay, the officer mounted a horse and galloped after the smugglers. Reaching the toll-house on the Hayle Causeway, he knocked up the toll-keeper and asked if any waggons had passed through. The toll-keeper – heavily bribed – said, 'No! I hab'n seen no waggons, nar doan't want to. What do 'ee want of waggons?' Without stopping to give an explanation, the officer wheeled his horse round again, and dashed off towards Penzance, to which town he assumed the waggons must have gone. Arriving there, however, he could learn nothing of the smugglers, and eventually returned to St Ives an angry and disappointed man.

He then turned his attention to Capt Williams' smack, the *St George*, laying at anchor in the Bay. Going on board, he found no one there except a foreign seaman – some accounts say he was the cabin boy. Everyone else, including Capt Williams, had, of course, gone off to Redruth with the waggons. Prior to his departure, the master had thoroughly schooled the young German in how he should behave if anyone questioned him. Consequently, the officer's enquiries concerning the whereabouts of the captain, and the nature of the cargo, were all met with the one answer, 'I don't know.' Threats, bribery and cajolery only resulted in violent head-shaking and gesticulation, much muttering in German, and that solitary English phrase, 'I don't know.' So well did he play his part that the officer eventually left, no wiser than when he had begun his investigation. The name of this cabin boy was Schmidt; he was born at Memel, East Prussia, in 1831, but ran away to sea at about the age of twelve, and so eventually formed a part of Capt Williams' smuggling crew. He was threatened with the rope's end if he gave away any information to the Customs authorities; and it was this which made him so keen to keep his master's secret!

However, although no evidence could be unearthed, the local Customs officers found a pretext for detaining the *St George* in consequence of the name of her stern being partially hidden, and her ship's boat having neither the name of captain or vessel, as required by law.

A brief account of the incident with the waggons, and the arrest of the smack, appeared in the local press plus a remarkable letter written by Capt James Williams himself, complaining of the way in which he and his vessel were being treated by the authorities. It is, indeed, one of the very few documents written by a smuggler which have come down to us.

The fact that he wrote and published such a letter at this time shows what a bold man Capt Williams must have been. It is also most cleverly worded. Capt Williams insinuated that the coastguard who attempted to stop his waggon had been tipsy, and had therefore not really known what passed. Also, whilst complaining of the detention of his ship, he nowhere actually denied being involved in a smuggling transaction. True to the generally honourable traditions of the smuggling 'profession', the master of the *St George* scorned to tell a lie about his activities on that night. It reads as follows:

Sir, A paragraph appeared in the West Briton *paper of last week, headed 'Smuggling', and also that a vessel named the* St George, *of Bristol, has been detained at the port of St Ives by the Customs, in consequence of the name in her stern not being sufficiently plain. I beg to acquaint you that I am the master of the above smack, and that I brought her to an anchor in St Ives Bay on Saturday morning the 31st of May last, for the purpose of taking in some baskets of fish, being at the time bound up channel. To my surprise, on Monday she was brought into the port by the Custom-house officers and Coastguard.*

The general belief in this town and neighbourhood is, that as one of the Coastguard, named Cock, was rambling from a public house late on Saturday night, he fancied he met a waggon loaded with contraband goods, and in his attempt to stop the waggon was either knocked down, or from some other cause fell under the waggon. This circumstance has caused the detention of my vessel, as at that time she was the only one in the the bay. The vessel is still under an arrest, and I very much doubt whether I shall not lose the confidence of my employers unless this business is thoroughly explained; how far they have a right to detain the ship I am at a loss to conceive. Had this occurred in any other port I should with my crew be in a state of very great distress. I am a native of this port and am in consequence thrown upon my friends for my daily bread...

This letter appeared on the 13th; and possibly as a result of the publicity given to the case the *St George* was released from custody of HM Customs on the 16th. However, Capt Williams did not immediately leave St Ives – perhaps through contrary winds; and on the morning of the 20th his vessel was again detained after a quantity of spirits had been 'crept up' by the Custom House officers. A piece of chain, and the rope attached to the tubs, were found to correspond with those on board the smack and as a result of this new development Capt Williams was brought to trial, accused of smuggling. The German cabin boy, still being very much in fear of the rope's end, again played his part to perfection, feigning ignorance of everything that had occurred on the night of May 31st, so that the case collapsed.

Traditions of this very interesting affair are still current at St Ives. The young cabin boy, who served his master's interests so well, settled in the town, where his descendants still reside. He was generally known as 'Prussian Bob,' and lived to a good age. Capt Williams bore the soubriquet of 'Old Worm', whilst the clever role played by the cabin boy was commemorated by the appellation 'Old Worm's Fool'.

Even today, when a St Ives person is suspected of pretending ignorance of some matter for an ulterior reason, he is liable to be accused of being 'an Old Worm's Fool'. But not all who use this expression are aware of the strange story which lies behind it.

Old Dutchy

During the latter half of the last century large numbers of fishing boats left Cornwall in June and July for the North Sea herring season, returning to their home ports again in September. Every fisherman would bring back with him some presents for his family and friends. One of the most popular for the children was a stick or two of Scarborough rock; whilst for their elders there were often sets of earthenware – Whitby pans – shallow dishes used for domestic purposes – and similar articles.

In the early 1880s, however, many of the men started to bring home expensive bottles of perfume and packets of good quality tobacco, which were duly distributed among their delighted kinsfolk. As fishermen were a somewhat impecunious lot, much surprise was occasioned at their apparent sudden access of wealth. The explanation was, however, a simple one. The North Sea fishing grounds had been invaded by a number of Dutch 'coopers' – floating shops – from whom uncustomed goods could be purchased at only a fraction of the prices ashore. These transactions took place on the high seas, where the Customs authorities were powerless to interfere; although it was, of course, an offence to bring such goods ashore. However, the fishermen had few scruples on this point, smuggling having never been regarded as a very serious sin in Cornwall.

For a time everything went well with these 'free traders'. They and their friends maintained a discreet silence, and the local Customs officers seemed to have no suspicion of what was going on. However, the amount of tobacco illicitly landed at St Ives eventually became so great that the shopkeepers began to notice a marked decline in their sale of it; and one of them, incensed by his serious loss in trade, informed the authorities what was going on.

This was during the summer of 1884. The fishing fleet was then still away; and the Chief customs officer of St Ives and the Coastguards made preparations to 'rummage' them on their return. The first boat to arrive – the *Charles* – came in on a Monday morning in early September, a few days ahead of the main part of the fleet. She was promptly boarded by a commissioned boatman of the Coastguard, who discovered two half-pounds of tobacco on board; and the boat's owner was duly brought before the magistrates, charged with smuggling. The bench inflicted a fine of £1 0s 6d. and

5s. 6d. costs, with the alternative of one month's imprisonment; but the money was immediately paid.

The case caused consternation at St Ives, as it was the first of its kind ever brought against a local fisherman. Anxiety now began to be felt by the relatives of the hundreds of men who at that very moment were sailing home from the North. There seemed, at first, no means of warning them of the hot reception prepared against their return. Then someone proposed sending a small boat out in the offing to inform the fishermen, as they approached, of the danger.

At first this measure proved highly effective. As the boats came in, one by one, during the rest of that week, they were warned by the small boat to dispose of any contraband on board before entering harbour – presumably by throwing it overboard. By Friday September 12, however, the boats were arriving in greater numbers; and probably because of this, two of them – the *Majestic* and *Matilda* – failed to receive warning of the rummage that was proceeding in the harbour. Accordingly, when these boats came in, the coastguards, in searching them, 'drew blood'. On board the *Majestic* they discovered three bottles of perfume belonging to three young members of the crew. No attempt had been made to conceal the articles. After the Coastguard had impounded the bottles the fishermen were allowed to go about their business, but later in the day they were told to come to the police station.

Word quickly spread of what was happening; and a crowd of sympathisers soon gathered round the doors of the old Town Hall in the Market Place (where the police court and 'lock-up' were situated); and whenever a coastguard appeared, he was greeted with groans and jeers. The three men were remanded until Wednesday; but it was then learned that one of the *Matilda*'s crew had been taken to the Custom House on an accusation of attempting to smuggle tobacco and cigars. After considerable delay he, too, was brought to the Town Hall by PC James Bennetts, St Ives' famous 'only policeman' in the Victorian era, followed by hundreds of people, who made the streets ring with cheers for the smugglers and groans for the obnoxious coastguards. This young fisherman was, however, also soon released, like the others, on remand.

Towards evening the main body of the North Sea fleet began to appear outside the harbour. During that night and the following morning no less than forty vessels arrived. It was a thrilling spectacle to see these sturdy sailing craft come home again to St Ives after several months' absence; and on this occasion a new note of drama was added by the events which had occurred earlier that day. A large crowd had assembled on the quays and landing places; and as one after another of the fishing boats ran in, they were greeted with loud cheers. Owing to the arrival of so many vessels in so short a time, the small staff of coastguards were unable to make an effective search and in fact may also well have been intimidated by the large and hostile crowd. At all events, no further discoveries of contraband were made.

The trial of the accused fishermen took place on September 17th. It was argued by the defending solicitor that excisable goods on coasting vessels must be declared at the Custom House within 24 hours of arrival in port. The *Majestic*, however, had been searched as soon as she grounded, without giving the crew any opportunity of declaring the perfume. The perfume, moreover, had not been concealed. The charge brought against them would consequently seem to be without foundation. The magistrate's verdict was that he could find no evidence of an attempt to land the goods illegally, and the cases would therefore be dismissed, was received by an outburst of applause from members of the public who had packed the small courtroom, all friends of the fishermen.

When silence was at last restored, the mayor appealed for order, and complained in strong terms at the absence of the other magistrates who should have been present to assist in trying the cases. These gentlemen had doubtless kept away to avoid the odium that would have fallen on them had they been obliged to convict, for public sympathy was entirely with the accused.

The case of the member of the *Matilda*'s crew charged with

attempting to land illegally a quantity of Cavendish tobacco and cigars was then proceeded with. The magistrates here could not agree on a verdict. The mayor gave his view that as the goods had not been removed from the fishing boat into the punt, the defendant could not be convicted of illegal landing. His colleague did not concur with this opinion; so the magistrates' clerk entered a record in the Magistrates' book: 'The Bench not agreeing, the case is virtually dismissed, without prejudice to either party'.

The St Ives fishermen had thus come off very well in their 'brush' with the Customs, their only casualty being the conviction of the unfortunate skipper of the *Charles*. There can be no doubt that the Customs men in their zeal to check the landing of contraband had acted with undue precipitancy, bringing a series of charges which could not be substantiated. By using a little more cunning they might have been more successful; but even so, the strong community spirit which prevailed among the fishermen must have made his task very difficult.

The effect of these cases was to make the fishermen more circumspect in their choice of presents when returning from the North Sea voyage. Some years later, however, a new kind of temptation was placed in their way. One of the coopers, registered in Holland, and popularly known as *'Old Dutchy'*, began to anchor outside St Ives Bay, where she was visited by local fishermen, who made extensive purchases of duty-free rum and tobacco from her stores which they brought ashore concealed amongst their gear. These transactions usually took place at night; and for some time the Customs officers, though highly suspicious, could obtain no definite proof as to what was going on.

At last, in desperation, the Customs authorities decided to send spies among the fishermen to find out what was happening. These newcomers were very friendly, liberal with their tobacco, and always ready to stand drinks. As a result, they were soon in possession of all the information required.

A raid was thereupon carried out on the houses of those known to be trafficking in the smuggled goods, and a large quantity of tobacco came to light, hidden away in cellars, lofts, outhouses, and other unlikely places. At one house, in the Warren, some tobacco had been concealed in a bedroom. When the Revenue men arrived and announced they were going to search the premises, the lady of the house said she had no objections, but would they allow her to tidy the bedroom first, as the bed was not made? They graciously consented, whereupon she rushed upstairs and hurled the tobacco through the window on to the rocks below. When the officers had left, after finding nothing, the tobacco was retrieved and secreted in a much safer hiding place until the affair had blown over.

Old Dutchy also spent some time off the Scilly Isles selling goods to the fishing boats. The lugger *Hugh Bourne* boarded the Dutchman there on one occasion and purchased considerable quantities of roll tobacco and perfume. These goods were stowed away in a secret locker aboard the fishing vessel. This locker could be opened without keys or handles, the method of doing so being known only to one or two members of the crew. On reaching St Ives, the *Hugh Bourne* was boarded by the St Ives customs officer, who made a thorough search, but failed to find any contraband. Coming on deck, he told the skipper that he knew perfectly well there were smuggled goods aboard, as the *Hugh Bourne* had been reported to him as having been in communication with *Old Dutchy* off Scilly. The skipper retorted that if there was any tobacco on board, there should be no great difficulty in finding it. The officer then resumed his search, but without result. Later, the articles of contraband were taken from the locker and brought ashore at Porthgwidden, concealed in baskets of mackerel. The mackerel were duly taken down over Dick's Hill to the harbour and sold in the usual way, but how the perfume and tobacco were disposed of is best left to the imagination.

As the 'searchers' were carrying out their raid, word quickly spread through the town, and those who had sufficient warning hid their tobacco in the safest places they could think of. Some relatives of the author are reputed to have concealed a large quantity of contraband in the roof of Zion (Countess of Huntingdon's) Chapel, in Fore Street. Large amounts of tobacco were buried on the Island, where some of it might still be found, if one only knew the right places to dig!

However, despite these stratagems, the authorities succeeded in making a good many seizures. Not wishing to be too severe on the fishermen, however, they permitted them to escape prosecution by paying duty on all tobacco found in their possession. Two innkeepers, also implicated in the affair, were later brought to trial. The ramifications of the smuggling were so widespread and feeling in the town running so high, that the Government deemed it prudent to station a gunboat at St Ives at the time of the trial. Accordingly, HMS *Renard* was sent round from Holyhead and dropped anchor in the bay the day before it was held, Commander Paton, the chief officer, subsequently attending the court proceedings in person. However, this precaution proved unnecessary, as everything passed off in an orderly fashion.

The first case heard was that brought against the proprietress of the ancient 'Sloop Inn', on the Wharf. In the face of the evidence arrayed against her in court, in the form of seized tobacco, the lady had no option but to plead guilty to both counts. The solicitor for the Customs thereupon consented to drop the second charge, for which the penalty was £20, if she consented to pay treble the duty and value on the tobacco involved in the other summons, to compromise the matter.

The landlord of the 'Sloop's' neighbour, the 'White Hart', was then charged with having on April 29 1898 – the day of the raid – on his premises *1lb 8 oz of Cavendish tobacco, with which had been mixed ten per cent of liquorice, and which was not enclosed in a label, contrary to the Manufactured Tobacco Act, 1863*. This defendant also pleaded guilty, saying the tobacco was bought for his own use, and not for sale.

There have been no prosecutions for smuggling at St Ives since that time, the authorities' show of force having finally convinced the fishermen that the game had become too dangerous to play.

Truro, Tobacco and Trade

Some incidents connected with smuggling actually took place in the landlocked port of Truro itself. For example, during the night of July 3 1800, a horse which had been previously seized from John Dunstone of Stithians for carrying two casks of smuggled brandy and gin was stolen from a stable 'situated in Kenwyn Street, near the borough of Truro'. The Commissioners of Customs later offered a reward of £20 for the detection of those responsible. Another robbery took place one night in March 1801. In this case, a cellar belonging to the port was broken open and twelve ankers of gin stolen. Three days later, however, ten of these were recovered through the vigilance of the Customs officers, a man called John Leane of Gwennap being apprehended. He was later sentenced, together with one James Marks, to seven years' transportation at the county assizes.

Tobacco was another commodity handled in great quantities by the Truro smugglers. A letter written from there by 'A Traveller' and published in the *Royal Cornwall Gazette* (October 27 1804) stated:

I had heard of the pitch to which smuggling was carried on in this county long before I saw it, but could not believe that such an unlawful traffic could be carried on with the degree of boldness and audacity that I now find it is. Lately passing through a neighbouring market town I found smuggled tobacco as publicly exposed for sale as any lawful commodity on the market. Indeed, a person could scarcely pass the place where it was selling without having the article publicly recommended to him with assurances of its goodness and cheapness, and many importunities to buy. On making enquiry in the town I was creditably informed many hundredweights of smuggled tobacco were sold there every market day.

Smugglers' caves and secret tunnels

Secret passages sound like something out of Enid Blyton but some really did exist.

The Tea Caverns at Newquay, are a very good example. These are situated near the Huer's House and consist of two caverns, an inner and an outer, separated by a chasm which the smugglers bridged by a plank. Tradition tells how when the Preventive men pursued the 'free traders' into their lair, they turned the plank round and precipitated them into the rough sea below, to sink or swim as best they could. The inner cave was elbow shaped and thus it could not be fired into. Here the men kept the lanterns used for signaling to ships in the bay if the coast was clear. The best China tea, landed and hidden in these caves, was later retailed in the neighbourhood for as little as 5 shillings a pound.

There was an even more remarkable smuggling cave or 'Vouggha' at Porthcothan, the small cove near Bedruthan. Here the cliffs tower up to 30 metres above the sea, whilst near their base the sea foams over chains of rocks and small islands. The cave was situated in the valley through which a stream runs down to the beach at Porthcothan. The Rev. S. Baring-Gould records that this tiny coombe was formerly a great harbour for smugglers. The cave entrance, carefully concealed, lay more than half-way down the steep slope of the hill. Just inside, notches were cut in the rock, into which a beam might be thrust to close the mouth, which was then filled in with earth and brambles drawn over it. Two metres from the entrance another gallery branched off to the right; this extended over a kilometre. to reach a cluster of cottages at Trevemedar, where it opened in one of the gardens.

It branched off from the main chamber at an acute angle to the south east, and was carried in a sweep through the rock, with air and peepholes at intervals. When Baring-Gould saw it in 1894, this tunnel was already choked in several places, but at the beginning of the last century it was still open throughout, and in active use. An old woman living nearby told him how her father had seen the Vouggha 'filled with casks of run spirits right chuck-full.'

The smugglers used to run their loads into Porthcothan, or, if the Preventives were on the watch, into the adjoining cove of Porthmear, which is hidden by the island of Trescore, drawn like a screen in front. They then rolled or carried the kegs either to the mouth of the Vouggha or Trevemedar, and concealed them in the big cave. The Preventive men never discovered the existence of the cave themselves, and apparently no one from the district informed on them! From Baring-Gould's description, it appears that the cave and tunnel were made expressly for smuggling – a remarkable circumstance, if true. He says it was cut out of the solid rock, and that the pick marks were distinctly traceable throughout. At the end, someone had cut his initials and the date, 1747.

Double dealing

There is the delightful story concerning a certain John Curgenven, who enterprisingly and unknowingly offered to sell smuggled tobacco and French brandy to some officers of the Customs at Truro, informing them that these goods were part of a cargo he had just landed. He produced three quarts, in two jars, and a bladder, as samples, and said he could supply any quantity of spirits at the far from moderate price of 24 shillings per gallon. Upon this, they took Curgenven into custody, and on searching him found a small measure and a funnel. The following morning he was taken before the

Collector, who examined him and also the seized spirits. It was then found that the alleged French brandy was in fact British brandy of a very inferior quality, which he had purchased at one of the inns in Truro the same day at 13 shillings per quart!

'In this manner', commented the local newspaper, 'are the buyers of that precious article, nine times out of ten, completely duped!'

A Smuggling Ghost Story

Polperro has its own smuggling ghost story, the village supposedly being haunted by a headless man driving a hearse. The Talland smugglers found difficulty in transferring their casks inland, as laden horses were searched and wagons were too noisy. When a small-pox epidemic broke out, however, 'Battling Billy,' landlord of the Halfway House Inn, conceived the idea of conveying his kegs in a hearse. This ruse worked well for a time, but then one night everything went wrong. He had landed a cargo of brandy which had to be removed by daylight, and the hearse would not hold it all.

When Billy turned up with a second hearse, his men, growing nervous, were ready to run away, but under the lash of his tongue they got the second consignment aboard. As the last keg was being loaded the Preventive men rode into Talland. 'If they shoot me dead, my body'll drive the load to Polperro,' swore Billy, leaping on the box; and lashing his horses he drove like a madman, shots flying around him. That night Polperro fishermen heard the hearse rattling over the cobbled street, and opening their doors were horrified to see that 'Battling Billy' had been shot through the neck, so that his head hung over one shoulder, but his arm still lashed the maddened horses on, until hearse, horses and corpse plunged over the quay into the harbour. Afterwards, the fishermen said they knew when the ghost of

'Battling Billy' was coming, and until he had passed they kept their doors shut and their backs to the window lest they should see him and suffer the death he brought in his wake.

Such wonderful pieces of nonsense were encouraged by the 'free traders' as it ensured that superstitious country folk kept indoors and didn't prey into their activities. One suspects they may even have concocted such stories themselves.

The rewards of smuggling

There were considerable rewards offered by the Preventive service for information about smuggling activities. This information of course had to lead to a conviction or the seizure of goods.

Smugglers in fact, often took advantage of these rewards to enrich themselves and defraud the government in a most ingenious fashion. In 1820, it was stated that smugglers were running goods from France purposely to be seized, as they could thereby obtain double their cost price. This was done in two ways. One was, by taking the kegs of spirits to a Custom House, stating that they had been picked up at sea; the other, by informing a Custom House officer where he might make a seizure on the coast.

Another ingenious practice was, if they made their destined coast late, or were chased, to sink the goods; and they found a vigilant watch kept up by Preventive officers for some time, so making it dangerous to take up the kegs, they would give information, perhaps through a third party, of where they were sunk, and this would entitle them to at least as much as the cost price in France. By the tricks the government was defrauded of immense sums, so turning what was meant as deterrent to smuggling into an encouragement.

Smuggling in Cawsand

The twin villages of Cawsand and Kingsand, lying just inside Penlee Point on the western side of Plymouth Sound, were formerly noted as important centres of lawful fishing and unlawful smuggling, the two occupations being closely interlinked. The popularity of Cawsand with the 'free traders' is explained mainly by its proximity to Plymouth, which provided a large and profitable market for their goods.

It might be thought, the proximity of a great naval port, Devonport, with 'men-of-war' constantly going and coming, and a large staff of customs officers, to say nothing of the presence of an officer and several men in their very midst, and a revenue cutter or two at anchor in the bay would act as a deterrent. But, as a matter of fact, these obstructions only gave additional zest to smuggling, and for many years the business went on as merrily as ever, a large proportion of the Cawsand fishermen occupying themselves with little else.

The great period of smuggling at Cawsand lay mostly in the post-Napoleonic years, when a large number of released privateersmen and naval personnel found a new outlet for their peculiar skills in contraband running. But the 'trade' had been flourishing there long before then.

Women smugglers

In 1799 a traveller called Lipscombe visited Cawsand and wrote a curious description of the women smugglers of the place:

In going down the hill, towards Kingsand, we met several females, whose appearance was so grotesque and extraordinary, that I could not imagine in what manner they had contrived to alter their natural shapes so completely; till, upon enquiry, we found that they were smugglers of spirituous liquors; which they were at that time conveying from their cutter at Plymouth, by means of bladders fastened under their petticoats; and, indeed, they were so heavily laden that it was with great apparent difficulty they waddled along.

In 1804 the Collector at Plymouth described Cawsand as one of the worst places for smuggling in the whole district. He estimated that 17,000 small casks of spirits were smuggled every year into the village from inward bound vessels before clearing Customs at Plymouth. But it was the Peace of 1815 which really gave the 'free traders' their great opportunity. One important factor in their success was the type of fishing vessel in use at Cawsand, half-decked vessels possessing excellent sailing qualities, and just of the right size for bringing a typical cargo of about a hundred casks across the Channel.

Sinking the catch

Cawsand became, indeed, the headquarters of smuggling in the west for a period of about twenty years. Eventually with the development of the coastguard service the smugglers here, as elsewhere, found it necessary to sink their casks offshore, retrieving them later in small boats to minimise the risk of detection.

At a later period still, the increasing vigilance of the coastguard drove the smugglers further out from the coast, and vast quantities of goods were sunk as far out as the Eddystone lighthouse. The final phase was reached in the 1830s and 40s when the steadily growing risk of seizure obliged the operators to employ French vessels, which were immune from interception by the revenue cruisers outside territorial waters.

An interesting reference to a specific instance of the sinking of tubs around the Eddystone was published in a Cornish paper in April 1817. This stated that His Majesty's cutter *Dwarf* had carried into Plymouth 388 ankers of contraband spirits which she had crept up off the dreaded reef. With 64 brought in a few days before, this made a total of 452 ankers recovered there within the space of a week.

This record shows, incidentally, that the practice of sinking cargoes here started earlier than is generally supposed; no doubt the smugglers found this place eminently suitable for the purpose, as bearings and distances could so easily be taken from the lighthouse.

Dangers of smuggling

The Cawsand, preventives were involved in an exciting affair on the night of June 7 1831. At about half past eleven, Foot, the Preventative officer, and four of his men intercepted a large party of smugglers, nearly thirty in number, at Sheviock. They called on them to surrender the kegs they were carrying, but without effect. The smugglers were armed with bludgeons, and when the coastguards tried by force to seize the kegs, they fought them off. Foot and his men fired on them, and it was thought that several smugglers must have been wounded. Indeed, it was believed one must have been killed, as the ball entered his mouth and he dropped. The smugglers said, 'Come, let us take up the poor fellow,' and they then moved off. It was not known whether the party was composed of people from the neighbourhood or more distant parts. Some appeared to be seafaring men.

Stories of this kind underline the dangers which smugglers continually ran in the pursuit of their calling. When to these are added the hazards of landing goods at night in small coves and inlets, and scrambling up precipitous cliffsides burdened with kegs where a slip meant almost certain death, the question must be asked, whether the game was really worth the candle. For the men who merely organised the 'runs' it very often was, their profits being high and quickly earned. But for the hired crews and carriers who actually ran the gauntlet of Revenue cruisers and Preventive boats, it was a very different story.

No doubt they were tolerably well rewarded for their work, though they might have earned comparable wages in honest employment without running any risks at all. But it was these very risks, which were probably the greatest lure. Smuggling was, above all, a great adventure, an occupation in which men could display those qualities of initiative, quick-wittedness and daring which find so little outlet in normal living.

It is for the exercise of such admirable virtues that the Cornish smuggler lives on in legend and story; his motives may have been sordid and censurable, but his manner was always admirable and brave.